Why does God allow
NATURAL DISASTERS?

Why does God allow

NATURAL DISASTERS?

David Pawson

http://tppress.com

Published in The United States of America by
True Potential Publishing, Inc.
PO Box 904 Travelers Rest, SC 29690
http://tppress.com

This edition published by special arrangement with Terra Nova
Publications International Ltd
PO Box 2400 Bradford on Avon Wiltshire BA15 2YN

Why Does God Allow Natural Disasters? and other True
Potential Publishing books can be purchased in bulk by
churches, ministries and other organizations for evangelical,
educational or business promotional use. For information
please write Special Markets Department PO Box 904
Travelers Rest, SC 29690 or send your request via e-mail to:
info@tppress.com.

ISBN 978-0-9818961-4-4
Library of Congress Control Number: 2008906164

Cover design by Chelsey Corn

Printed in the USA

PREFACE

This book is based on a series of televised talks which I delivered following the Asian tsunami.

Originating as it does from the spoken word, its style will be found by many readers to be somewhat different from my usual written style. It is hoped that this will not detract from the substance of the biblical teaching found here.

As always, I ask the reader to compare everything I say or write with what is written in the Bible and, if at any point a conflict is found, always to rely upon the clear teaching of scripture.

David Pawson

Contents

1

IS GOD TO BLAME?

There have been many major disasters, and they have often led to the question being asked, by the press and in many minds, 'Where was God in this?' So I have addressed that question, which arose most widely at the time of the Asian tsunami and after the 9/11 disaster, when the Twin Towers of New York were destroyed.

What a difference there was between the two events! The tsunami (which I call '26/12') was by far the more destructive disaster, killing fifty times as many people as 9/11, damaging far more property and directly affecting many nations. But the biggest difference between the two tragedies was that the tsunami was not caused by human beings, whereas 9/11 was directly caused by people. So the tsunami was what the insurance companies call an 'act of God'. I am not sure that that means a lot these days, except that it is something we cannot insure against because it has no human cause. The expression 'act of God' seems to be to most people as meaningless as swearing on a Bible in a

1

court of law that you will tell the truth. These are among the vestiges of our godly past.

* * * * *

Initially we will focus on the Asian tsunami, but many of our observations will be seen to apply equally to other kinds of natural disaster.

Nowadays we witness such events on television. As we see them happen, so their horror quickly comes home to us and we are made aware of the human needs that are waiting to be met following the catastrophic event.

First there are great physical requirements. There is need for medical aid to the wounded, for burial of the dead, for food, water and shelter. There was an outpouring of aid from the whole world into the Indian Ocean area where the tsunami took place. But those physical needs very quickly give way to emotional needs. There is the shock and trauma. Counsellors were needed for those who are suffering from what was, quite literally, a shock wave. After that shock starts to subside, the next emotion to be dealt with is grief. At such times we feel very deeply for those who lose loved ones and those who are waiting for news of their families. I am then reminded of the times in World War Two when somebody would bring a telegram which said 'Missing in action'. Often the people concerned would never find out what had actually taken place. This happened to my cousin. She escaped with her two sons from Malaya when the Japanese came in. But for years she did not know what happened to her husband. She did not know whether she was a widow. For years she had to live with this ignorance, which was even harder to bear than would have been the case had she been told then (as she later discovered) that her husband had been killed by the Japanese.

So after shock comes sorrow and grief —and then anger. After every disaster there is anger. People look for a scapegoat, someone to blame, on whom they can vent their anger. That anger needs to be dealt with. In the case of a natural disaster, of course, the 'scapegoat' is often God himself. I heard many people blaming God for the tsunami. They cannot blame any human being. They blamed the then Prime Minister for not breaking his holiday and coming back to take charge of the situation. But they knew full well that there was no human being to blame for the event itself. So God became their scapegoat.

After every disaster, people are either drawn nearer to God or driven further from him. One or the other is bound to happen to all of us, even if we were not personally involved. So there is a third need. There are the physical needs, such as food, water, medicine and shelter; there are the emotional needs, which arise from shock, grief and anger. But then we come to what I want to call the intellectual needs. There is a need in every human being to make sense of what happens, to ask deeper questions, and we move from the first and second needs into the third as people ask these big questions: How did this come to happen? What caused it?

Naturally, there is a scientific answer to this, so we know what happened. We know that two tectonic plates rubbed against each other, got caught, and the movement stopped for a bit and then suddenly was released. The energy released was so enormous that it sent a gigantic wave around the whole Indian Ocean. Do you know that it even wobbled planet earth two inches on its axis? So the whole earth moved. It was a gigantic thing. But we know how it happened. And of course the reason for asking the question 'how did it happen?' is so that in future we may avoid it, or escape it, or at the very least have a warning. The sad thing is that the Pacific Ocean has such a warning system about tsunamis, but the Indian Ocean (being in a poorer part of the world and farther from America) did not have that. That is the first kind of question that the intellect needs to ask and answer.

But there is an even more important question that many people's minds grapple with, and need to be satisfied about, and that is: 'Why?' —not just 'How did this happen?', but, 'Why did it happen?' We need to find a 'reason' for it because the thing we cannot cope with is senseless suffering — wasted suffering; wasted life; wasted property. So we want to know whether there is any reason behind it. Is there any sense in it? Or do we have to live with something that has no reason at all and which therefore leaves us suspended in our mental questions? In the aftermath of any disaster it may seem to be heartless to discuss such objective questions. Nevertheless, I believe it is necessary, if only for the reason that God is being blamed. I want to defend the truth about God. I believe in him. I trust him. And I believe a lot of blame is wrongly attached to God in this kind of situation.

2

HAVE CHRISTIANS FOUND THE ANSWER?

In what follows I want to deal with some of the wrong answers that have been given to this question, even by Christians and church leaders. So what follows here may seem a little negative, but I want to clear the decks for the true answer, what I believe is the Bible's answer to this appalling question, this deep question: 'Where was God in all this?'

Now the fact that we must come to terms with is that we live in a fragile (and even hostile) environment. We are clinging to life by our fingertips. We are told that the whole vast universe is expanding rapidly, and in that entire universe planet earth is as a tiny speck of interstellar dust —and there are asteroids out there that could hit us any moment and deal with the human race in the way that it dealt with the dinosaurs, which have gone! Coming to planet earth itself, we live in this tiny, wafer-like atmosphere around the planet. It is so thin that if we go ten miles up we are dead and if we go ten miles down we are dead. Do you know that no man has been into space yet, because you cannot live in space? The only way we can get men up there is to give them a capsule of earth with enough of earth's air and water and food in it, and then they can go out into space. But they haven't gone into space. They have taken earth with them. One American astronaut was asked whether he had met God out there. He smilingly said, "I would have done if I stepped out of my spacesuit." We are trapped in this tiny thin layer around planet earth, and already we know how delicately it is balanced. Global warming is a threat. The weather in the 1970s took a turn for the worse and now it is increasingly erratic.

Life is becoming less and less secure. And now we have learned that the earth beneath our feet is not solid. We are floating on plates of rock called tectonic plates. These are colliding with each other and slipping under each other and they are being renewed on one side and dissolved again on the other.

So life is increasingly fragile and increasingly hostile. It is really quite amazing that any of us are surviving under such conditions. This raises the urgent question: is there anybody up there in charge? Is there anybody in control of our universe, or is it just running in its own way, haphazardly, and anything could happen anywhere? If this universe is an accident then it is not surprising that accidents will happen. Is it a matter of chance or choice that we are here? Are we indebted to something, some force, or someone? That is the most basic philosophical question that man can ask. It has been discussed for many centuries and there are a great many answers to it. Is there anyone in charge? Is there a God?

In what follows we will look at some of the different answers that have been given, because with some of those answers there is no problem with tsunamis or earthquakes or any other natural disaster. With others the problem becomes very acute.

ATHEISM

First let us take the answer called atheism. This says that there is no God, and that this universe evolved by chance. We are here by chance, in other words by luck. To atheism, therefore, there is no problem about natural disasters. That is the way it is. That is the way it has evolved. We must accept any disaster, live with it, try to survive through it. But there is no problem. There is no intellectual 'Why?' because that question becomes irrelevant if there is no-one in charge —if there is no God.

AGNOSTICISM

There's another *–ism* like that, which is very close to it, called 'agnosticism', which means the 'don't knows', people who do not know whether there is a God or not; people who just say, 'Well, there might be or there might not be.' Now to them there is no problem either. If anything, natural disasters tend to drive agnostics nearer to atheism rather than theism which believes in God. But on the whole they do not have a real problem. They are not asking that question.

POLYTHEISM

Then there is the strange *–ism* called polytheism, which says there are many gods controlling our environment, and natural disasters are the result of some of those gods falling out with other gods. When you believe in many gods you can believe that these disasters are the result of quarrelling among them.

DUALISM

Then we have dualism, and this is more common. Dualism tends to believe in two gods: one bad and one good. If there are two gods up there, and one is responsible for all the good things that happen and the other responsible for all the bad things, you have no problem, because that is the way it is. Some Christians tend to get quite near to dualism when they think the devil is as powerful as God, and they attribute all the bad things that happen to the devil and all the good things that happen to God. That can be a form of dualism. But the devil is a creature like us. He is not the creator. He is not all-powerful, and we must not attribute everything 'bad' to him, though we can attribute quite a bit.

MONOTHEISM

Monotheism is the belief that there is one God, and now we begin to have a problem. If there is only one God, then he must be responsible for natural disasters. So it is not atheists and agnostics and polytheists and dualists who have the problem, but monotheists certainly do. If you believe that this is a *uni*verse (because there is only one person in charge of it) then he must be held responsible for what happens in it. But even within monotheism we have a further question that we have to sort out. If there is one God, there is not a problem if that God is bad. At best he does not care about us, or at worst he enjoys seeing us suffer —and I have heard people say both of those things. And if you believe that the one deity in charge of this universe is a bad god, then there is no problem. When he does bad things that is because he is bad. But supposing he were to be (like us) a mixture of good and bad —and that he does both good things and bad things. Well, again, there is no problem. It just means that when we have a bad disaster he is having a bad day, he is in a bad mood. If you believe that God is both bad and good – and sometimes one, sometimes the other – then there is no problem.

We have now reached the heart of the intellectual problem, which is this: Christians believe in a God who is totally, thoroughly good, with no badness in him whatsoever. Now we have a real problem. How could a God in control of everything allow such bad things to happen? You see, what I am trying to say is this: a person who says 'I've got a problem, why did God allow this?' has already assumed two things: that God is good; and that he is Almighty. Those are two things that Christians believe, which the Bible teaches, and so only those who assume those two things have an intellectual problem with natural disasters.

To put it very simply, if God is all-powerful and all-loving, then how can such things happen in which there is so much suffering? That is the problem in a nutshell. We are at the heart of it now. Only those who believe those two things about God have a problem to wrestle with. Because I am a Christian and because I believe the Bible, I have that problem, and I have to find an answer to it.

3

WHAT IS GOD REALLY LIKE?

If the question is *If God is all-powerful and all-loving, then how can such things happen in which there is so much suffering?* then we need to be aware that there are a number of wrong answers which have been given by Christians, even by church leaders.

In the days which followed the Asian tsunami I listened to the broadcasts and studied the newspapers, hoping to hear a clear explanation from a Christian. But I did not hear one. Maybe I had not been listening to the right broadcasts or reading the right newspapers, books or articles. Nevertheless, I was grateful for the opportunity to work through to what I believe is a satisfactory explanation of natural disasters. But first we will concentrate on the wrong answers that are given. And I want to say why I believe they are wrong. They may have an element of truth in them, but in the last resort they do not satisfy the big question in my mind. I need to have an answer to the question 'Why?' that is satisfying in two ways: first to my mind, and second to my conscience. I need both because I am a human being who thinks and I am a human being with a conscience that knows the difference between right and wrong. So are you. You have a mind that puzzles over things, and which gets bewildered. You have a conscience that tells you when you are doing something less than your best or something positively wrong. Now we could think of explanations that are mentally satisfying to my mind but which do not satisfy my conscience. They seem to be wrong in some way. Let me deal then with three wrong answers that do not satisfy me.

1. The first that many Christian preachers give is this: Suffering is a mystery. You will never understand it. You cannot understand it because you are not God, and God's ways are so much higher than our ways, and God's thoughts are so much higher than our thoughts that we will never understand why he does it. We must therefore trust him to believe that he has good reasons for himself which he has chosen not to share with us and so we cannot understand it. Our little minds cannot grasp it.

There is an element of truth in this. One book in the Bible really seems to say that this is the case, and that is the Book of Job. Job suffered greatly. He lost his family, lost his business, lost his property. Finally he lost his health. It was all taken from him. And he could not understand why. He was quite sure he did not deserve it, and that was the moral problem that he had. He knew that he had not been very wicked. His friends were quite sure he had. We call them 'Job's comforters', and they came and said to him, 'You must have sinned pretty badly to have all this happen to you.' They were wrong, and God said they were wrong. But

12

when you read the Book of Job one thing hits you: God never told him why. And, right at the end, God really hammered him with a most extraordinary argument. He said, 'Job, I want you to meditate on the hippopotamus.' Now that is the cure for depression, according to the Bible. Meditate on the hippopotamus. When you are puzzled, when you are depressed, when you do not know what is happening, think about the hippopotamus. Why? Do you know why God made the hippopotamus? Of course you don't!

Then he went on to talk about the crocodile. 'Job, do you know why I created that?' Job you're getting a bit too big for your boots asking all these 'why?' questions.

Job finally surrendered and said, 'God I shouldn't have said what I said. I shouldn't have questioned you like that. I'm just man and you're God.' Actually, that was enough for God to restore all that Job had lost. But that is not the whole story. I believe that if we resort to saying 'suffering is always a mystery' we will never really answer satisfactorily the questions that people are asking. So let us go a bit further.

'It is useless to ask,' say some. 'You should not ask "Why?" You will just drive yourself into frustration, even bitterness, because you won't get the answer. God isn't telling. So it's a pointless thing to do.' Some Christians have gone even further and said it is a wrong thing to do. 'Who do you think you are, questioning God?' Of course we need to remember – here is the element of truth in this – that God is not accountable to me. He does not need to justify what he does to me and tell me what he can do or cannot do. I must not tell him what he can and cannot do. That would be sheer impudence. The Bible calls it the clay arguing with the potter. We would be out of place.

Yet this idea that suffering is a mystery, that it always will be, that little me will never understand, leaves me unsatisfied for a number of reasons. First of all, God wants me to love him. More than that, he has commanded me to love him. But if he does not explain these disasters to me he is not encouraging me to love him, is he? He is not encouraging me to trust him when he does things like this, and it blows my mind. If I am to love God, then he must be a God whose ways I can, to some extent, understand. He must share with me the reasons why he does things so that I can understand his mind and will relate to him.

Jesus said to his disciples, 'I'm telling you all this because you are my friends.' God wants friends. He wants me to be his friend. Abraham was his friend. With a friend you explain why you are doing something that hurts your friend. Of course you do.

Then there is another reason why I believe this is not the full answer, and it is simply this. What can I learn from disasters if God does not tell me anything about them? What lessons can I learn? What improvements can I make in my life? What adaptation can I make to his laws and his love if he does not explain anything to me? The third reason why I found this answer (suffering is a mystery and we'll never know) to be wrong is this: Throughout the Bible, God is explaining things to people, and when disaster comes he explains why it comes. In fact, to the prophet

Amos he said: 'I never send anything to my people Israel without warning them first.' It is only just and fair of God to do this. If disaster is coming he will tell us why. God is constantly explaining himself in the Bible, from beginning to end. That is the kind of God he is. He wants us to know. And the word 'mystery' to God is not what it means to us. The word 'mystery', when it occurs in scripture, means something that God has now told us but something that we could never have understood for ourselves, something we could never have discovered. For example, Paul talks in the letter to the Romans about the mystery that God will one day save all the Jewish people. That is something that nobody could have found out for themselves. Nobody would have guessed it. Yet Paul says, 'I am telling you a mystery', and the best translation of the word 'mystery' in the Bible is *a secret that God has now revealed*, something that only he knew and understood, but which now he is sharing with us and which we can now comprehend.

This is the general picture of God in the Bible: a God who shares with us the reasons why he does things because he wants us to respond to them in the right way. Now put all those reasons together. And here we have a real blockage to the idea that all suffering will always be a mystery.

Now I know there are some things we do not understand and pray one day we will —when we see God as he really is, see things from his point of view and begin to understand. For example, in my own case, my wife was dying of cancer but God had mercy and healed her, and she is still with me twenty years later. But my daughter died a few years later of leukemia. This naturally raised a question in my mind: why did he heal my wife and take my daughter? I believe he has given me the answer to both questions, but nevertheless at the time I did not understand, and I had to wrestle with my thinking until I believed I was thinking God's way and not mine.

So the first wrong answer, I believe, is to say that natural disasters are a complete mystery. 'You will never understand. God may. And he may have his reasons, but he is not telling us and we must just accept.' It is a kind of resignation. It is a kind of fatalism. It is a kind of saying, 'It is God's will so I must just simply submit to his will.' That is being said by some religions, particularly Islam, and even some Christians: that when these disasters happen it is best to be quite stoic about them and say 'God's will be done', and keep calm and not get agitated about it. But that does not work with me.

2. Let us look now at a second wrong answer which I believe to be inadequate. And this is looking at all the good that comes out of disaster, as if to say that the good that comes out of it justifies the bad in it. It is an extraordinary argument, but we need to consider it. At the time, a disaster does not feel very good, but there is no doubt that afterwards there is a release of all that is best in human nature. There are sometimes wonderful stories of sacrifices made to save others, and we have seen examples of that in the press. Did you see the photograph of the woman who was dashing into the sea – straight for the big wave – to save her family when the tsunami struck? She could easily have drowned, but in fact her family were saved. But I heard of other cases where parents saved their children at the cost of their own lives. Self-sacrifice comes out at the time. And afterwards there is a wave of sympathy and support. In the case of the

tsunami this came from all over the world because so many countries were affected. (I was in Norway shortly after that event and heard that there were five hundred Norwegians missing, and next door, in Sweden, there were thousands still missing, unaccounted for.) The whole world was affected. But look at all the goodwill that has been released.

We live in a selfish, greedy world, where people are interested in bettering themselves. Suddenly, people become unselfish. Many give sacrificially. At great cost to themselves, they go to rescue people, to help serve them, to rebuild their lives, to rebuild their homes. There is so much good that is released that would never have been released but for the disaster. In other words, to use an old-fashioned word, *charity* is released. I know that word has a nasty taste to many, but the charity that was released by the tsunami, for example, is something of which we need to take notice. Normally selfish people act unselfishly and materialistic people think less about getting more material possessions and more about giving some to those who have none —clothes, and all kinds of other things. We are shaken out of our selfishness, giving instead of getting. The shock wave produces that immense reverse wave of goodwill. And people say that really explains the disaster: look what good has been done since!

Now of course we need to look at the whole picture. Following the tsunami I was shocked at some of the evil that has been released in human nature. There was looting – otherwise called stealing – in the ruins of cities and towns and villages. But there was even worse than that. I was horrified to hear that human beings are kidnapping orphan children who have lost the rest of their family, in order to sell them for adoption. Sri Lanka had to ban adoption for a time, to stop this dreadful trade. Then there were body snatchers who were stealing bodies so that they could receive compensation, claiming this was their loved one who had been earning bread for the family. So what comes out of people when natural disasters occur is by no means all good. A cynic might also say that the rush to help is a kind of collective insurance or that a motive is collective self-preservation. In other words, we may be the next to suffer and we would hope that then others will look to our needs as we have looked to theirs.

As I write, I reflect that there has once again been extensive flooding in Britain as well as in many other places around the world. Again, cynics are heard to suggest that the desire to help often stems from a kind of instinct for the preservation of our species. I say our species because there is little or no attempt to help to do something about the animals who perish or suffer (and the animal rights people talk about that quite vociferously).

So there is a downside. The biggest negative about such waves of human sympathy and desire to support is that they fairly quickly fade. Soon, any disaster is off the front pages of the newspapers. It is no longer the first item in news bulletins, on radio and television. As the interest and concern quickly fade, the world goes back to normal — back to its selfish greed; back to its materialism; back to all that has been deeply shaken. We have an amazing capacity for quick recovery from shocks and things that happen that we do not welcome.

There is another 'good thing' to come out of tragedy. I have very mixed feelings about it, but just as disaster produces a wave of charity it also produces a wave of unity. But this is not only a unity of nations (or even races), the extraordinary thing is people are welcoming a kind of unity of religions which is now being observed. Some time ago, I was watching *Songs of Praise*. This had always been a Christian television program, exclusively for Christian praise. Other programs on the BBC have for a long time now included other religions. *Thought For The Day* and the Sunday morning program *Sunday* have become multi-faith, and there is as much about Islam as Christianity on Sunday mornings. But *Songs of Praise* was kept for Christian praise to the Christian God. No longer. One Sunday, in the period following the tsunami, it began with a statement rejoicing that the tsunami had brought nations and religions together. For the first time ever, *Songs of Praise* was led by a Christian, a Muslim mullah, a Hindu priest and a Buddhist monk, and the praise songs were from all those religions in the one program. The whole program was a celebration of the 'unity' that the tsunami had brought to the religions of the world. Now I have to be honest with you and say that I have really mixed feelings about that. But the world would love to see the religions of the world united to serve the needs of the human race. I remember listening to a sermon by the Duke of Edinburgh (the only time I have heard him preach in a church) and his theme was very simple: it was an appeal to the world religions to unite to save wildlife and our environment.

That is what many in the church today would love to see — the different religions no longer arguing with each other, fighting with each other, but uniting to serve the needs of mankind. A 'humanitarian religion' would be very welcome to the world. We will look more closely at that idea later.

These then are the things that are being singled out by the public as positive benefits. Now what are they really saying? Are they trying to tell us that the good that comes out of a disaster justifies the bad in it? Are they actually arguing that God has deliberately done a bad thing in order to make us good, to bring out the better side of our nature? It certainly does that. But was God intending that and was it too high a cost? The loss of more than 250,000 lives to make the rest of us a bit better, to release in us the good? I have problems with that. I have no doubt at all that people show the better side of their nature when there is a disaster. At least, many of them do. Some do not. But most do, and I acknowledge that. But I do not think that justifies the bad thing, indeed it leads us to an extraordinary conclusion, namely that we are better than God, that God did a bad thing but we are doing so many good things as a result. You know, it is almost impudent to talk to God like that, in effect saying, 'God, we could run the world a good deal better than you do.' If we were in charge, we would not use that method to bring out the good in people! Somebody once told me, 'You know, every time you grumble about the weather you're complaining about the way God runs the world.' That really shook me. We are very good at criticizing God. We have a high view of our goodness and a low view of his badness. We will see later that in fact that is the very opposite of the truth. If we start thinking we are very good in our behavior in a disaster and God is very bad in causing it, then quite frankly we are in real difficulties, even delusions.

3. We now move on to the third explanation that some Christians give, and this really is an extraordinary one. Let us go back to the problem in its simplest form again:

If God is almighty, all-powerful, all-good and all-loving, why should these things happen? They should not happen. God could stop them, even if he started them. And God should not have started it anyway.

There are the two assumptions behind the question 'Where was God in this?' — that *he is almighty* and that he is *all-loving*. Now supposing one or other or even both of those assumptions is wrong? Then the problem becomes a very different problem. If God is not almighty, then there is not a problem. He could not have started it or stopped it. If God is not all-loving there is not a problem. Now this final wrong answer that I am dealing with here says that God is not all-powerful. I must give you another little lesson in philosophy, another lesson in two *–isms*, because you can believe in God in two different ways.

There is **theism**, which is the philosophy of the Bible, which holds that God created and controls our physical universe. He has created it in the beginning and he still controls it. But there is another philosophy called **deism**. A deist believes that God created the world but he no longer controls it. In deism the world is thought of like this: it is as though God made it like a big watch or clock which he wound up; and then he took his hands off it, and it goes on in the way he designed it to go on, and he cannot do anything about it. It is no longer in his control.

21

Even many people in churches are deists. They do not, for example, believe in miracles, because that would mean God interfering with the mechanism of the 'clock'. It was widely believed in a so-called scientific outlook that nature is a mechanism, a closed system, not open to anyone's influence. It is running on cast iron laws of its own, like the law of gravity —the laws of nature. And even God himself cannot interfere with those laws now. God made nature once, long ago. He wound it up and now nature goes on its own way. Deists would never ask God to change the weather, for example, because they would say he cannot do so. The weather is running on its own cast iron laws, and God himself is not almighty enough to interfere with it or to change it at his will.

Now from that point of view comes an answer to the problem which I believe is the wrong answer. Let me go back to a television program I was watching with my wife a year or two back under the title *Credo*, which means 'I believe'. It was one in a series of religious programs with that title. The interviewer was speaking with a bishop who was chairman of the Commission of the Anglican Church which had the task of revising the doctrine of the Church of England, bringing its beliefs up to date, adapting them for our modern era and our modern outlook. The interviewer, a lady who was not a Christian, said to the bishop, 'What are you going to change in Christian beliefs in the Church of England?'

The bishop replied quite openly, 'Oh, we must change our thinking about God.'

'In what way?' she asked.

And he said, 'We must realize that God is weak.' To make the point even stronger, he said, 'as weak as water'.

The interviewer was astonished, and said, 'Well, how do you imagine God? How do you think of him?'

And the dear bishop said this: 'I think we are all like an extended family, the human race, and in the extended family there is a grandmother. And while all the family go to work and solve the problems, and work hard to make their life pleasant, the grandmother's love holds the whole family together. And her love is the key to the unity of the family. They all love her and she loves them all while they do all the work.'

In utter astonishment, the interviewer said, 'But I thought God was a Father, not a grandmother?'

The bishop appeared not the slightest bit embarrassed, and she then asked, 'Do you think that this view of God will fill the churches again?'

He had the courage to say, 'I believe this will really bring people back to church when they realize how much God needs them.' Not how much they need God, but how much God needs them!

He was painting a picture of a weak god who was all-loving but could not do much himself and was relying on us to help him with the problems that we face. Now that is a relatively new view but it is now quite widespread.

In other words, when we ask about the problem 'If God is all-loving and all-powerful, how can such things happen?' this answer says he is *not* all-powerful. He is as much a victim of these disasters as we are. He cannot help them, and we cannot help them. It is really an extraordinary answer. Then, you might ask, what is the point of trying to get through to God when there is a disaster? What help could he be to us? And the answer given is: he can *sympathise* with us. He *feels* for us. And they quote a verse from the Old Testament: 'In all their afflictions he was afflicted.' They offer this 'sympathy'.

Now 'sympathy' means (*sym*) 'with' (*path*) 'suffer'. To *suffer with* people. It is to say, 'I really feel for you.' So this is the comfort that even Christian preachers offer. God is suffering with you. He feels for you. So then he will support you emotionally; because he is present with you in the suffering, he will stand by you and suffer with you.

I have heard many preachers talking like this following a natural disaster: 'Believe that God is with you in the suffering.' It is really saying, 'Believe he is with you in solidarity, and that solidarity should be the comfort that you need.' But I believe that that is terribly wrong, because the Bible does not paint God as a weak god who cannot do anything about the situation. The Bible is quite clear that God is God Almighty, Maker of heaven and earth, that he still controls them and that he can still step into nature and make it do things that it would not otherwise do. The

24

picture of God and the universe in the Bible is rather like a headmaster who has made a school timetable at the beginning of term and said that on Tuesday morning at ten o'clock it will be a French lesson. But being the headmaster he can, any Tuesday, step in and say it will not be French at ten o'clock, it will be mathematics. He is the headmaster. He is in control of the school. And although he gives these timetables for regular behavior he can at any time change the timetable. He can step in and exercise his authority.

That illustrates something of the picture of God and nature in the Bible. Nature has been given laws, as it were, and there is a 'timetable' for how nature behaves. But the Bible also tells us that God can at any moment step in and do something with nature that nature would not have done by itself: that he can do miracles; that he does do miracles. This can go against the 'laws' of nature. Jesus' walking on water is against the law of gravity, but he did it. This is a very different picture of God from that of him as weak and unable to do much except sympathise with us and say, 'Well, I'm with you, I'm alongside.' The latter is totally against my understanding of the Bible.

So perhaps we ought to be asking whether we are right in thinking of God as all-loving. I have already tried to tell you that it is only these two assumptions that create the problem. Only those who are thinking that God is *almighty* (all-powerful) *and all-loving* are the ones who have the problem. So, in a sense, anybody who asks the question 'What was God doing in the disaster?' is already making those two assumptions. I have already tried to say that the assumption that God is not all-powerful is wrong. (That is, if you believe the Bible to be God's word.)

In fact we are now faced with the other assumption, and we are going to have to question that. Is God all-loving? What do we mean by that? Is it the truth?

To refer to a point I have made elsewhere, all religions of the world could be wrong, but only one of them could be right. That is because there is such wide variation in what religions think God is really like that they are contradictory to each other. You cannot put all the religions of the world into one. You just cannot. They have such different views of God.

So the question is: which view is the real view? Which is the one true God? The Bible claims to be telling us about the one true God. And in both the Hebrew and Greek languages the word for *true* is the same as the word *real*. So the Bible is claiming to present us with *the only real God who exists, and no other.*

So that is why I say that all the religions of the world could be wrong about God but only one of them can be right, and every one of us has a big decision to make as to which God we are really going to believe in. Which 'God' is the only real one? We are talking about the God who is in charge of our universe, in control of it, who made it, and can still do with it whatever he wills. All-powerful.

But is he all-loving? There was an opinion poll in Britain not long ago, and people were asked, 'Do you believe in God?' Something like 67% percent said they believed in God. But that is an irrelevant statistic. It should have been followed up with the question, 'What kind of God do you believe in?' What is he really like? Is he all-loving?

Later we will look at this in more detail. But we are going to ask the question now: how can we find out what God is really like? What is his character like? What is his personality? What kind of God is he? How are we going to find out?

How would you find out what I am really like — or anybody else? You would find out by listening to what I said and watching what I did. And I hope you would find a consistency between those two things. I hope you would feel that David Pawson said and did the same things, that his personality is consistent, that he has integrity. Well God has that integrity. There is no contradiction whatever between what God says and what he does. And we Christians believe in the *living* God, which means that God is in this world and is saying and doing things. The Bible is the record of what he has said and done in our world of time and space. And when we study his deeds and his words (which usually explain his deeds and tell us why he did what he did), we shall get to know him as he really is. And we shall get some surprises — some shocks even. ***We shall find he does not always behave in what we would call a loving manner.***

We must ask: What does the Bible say about God? Is he bad, good, a mixture? What is he really like? And then we shall ask: What does God say about ourselves? And we shall I hope come to the conclusion that God is a good deal better than we thought he was, and we are a good deal worse than we thought we were. We shall ask what God is telling us about the future. One of the things we will find that he is telling us is that earthquakes are going to increase in size and strength, and we shall ask what the Bible says about earthquakes in particular.

We noticed earlier that one of the needs which surfaces following a natural disaster is *intellectual*. Our minds need to grapple with what has happened. We ask questions about it.

The first question we ask is 'How did it happen?' What caused the disaster? If we can understand what caused it, then maybe we can avoid the danger or even prevent it in the future. So science has to give the answer to the question 'How?' But there is a much bigger question that we are considering, and that is the question 'Why?' Science cannot tell us why. Science can tell us how the universe began, how we came to be here, but it cannot tell us why the universe is here and why we are here. We are into the realm of philosophy and religion when we ask this sort of question about why things happen.

Now we need an answer to the question 'Why?' that satisfies two parts of us. It needs to satisfy our *mind* and satisfy our *conscience*. The mind needs a rational answer to why these things happen, and the conscience needs a moral answer. In other words, we not only need a reason but we also need a good reason, if we are going to find a satisfactory answer. For example, suppose I told you that God had built into nature a mechanism that keeps the world population down and helps us to provide enough food for those who are left, and that such events as tsunamis are deliberately put there to reduce the population and keep it within manageable proportions. That would be a rational answer. It is a reason. But something in us rebels. It is not what we would call a good reason. It is not a moral reason. Actually, over two hundred years ago a clergyman called Malthus wrote a book about this, and said that poverty, disease and wars are all designed to keep the population explosion from becoming too great. I do not agree with that. It may satisfy reason but it does not satisfy conscience.

Let us recap, and review our discussion of the issue thus far. I have already defined the problem very carefully, pointing out that you only have a problem about natural disasters if you have already accepted three assumptions. The first is that there is only one God. If there are many gods, or if there is no god at all, there is no problem. But if you believe there is only one God then you have a problem. The second assumption is that he is all-powerful and that he can control what he has created; that he is in charge of nature. And the third assumption you need to make before you have a problem is that God is all-loving. I have also mentioned three answers which I am afraid Christians are giving —church answers which are less than satisfactory. The first was that suffering is a complete mystery. No-one understands why. God has not told us. The only thing you can do in the face of such disasters is to say it is God's will and that we must 'submit' to that. We shall only get ourselves into a panic if we try to find out why. Suffering is a mystery. We do not understand it. Maybe we will one day, but we don't now. That is not a satisfactory answer. It leaves the mind and the conscience searching for more answers.

The second wrong answer I mentioned was that such

disasters produce a lot of good — much goodwill. Think of how many selfish and greedy people in the world suddenly become unselfish, caring for others. What goodwill has resulted from some disasters. But that does not justify the bad event that led to the goodwill emerging. Indeed, if you think that way you come to the conclusion that we humans are a good deal better than God. He caused it, and we become good at helping each other after it. Not a few people think that we are better than God and we could manage the world a good deal better than he does, if only we were in charge. So that is not a very satisfactory answer either. A lot of good may come out of a disaster, but that does not justify it.

The third wrong answer I referred to was an extra-ordinary one, namely that God himself is too weak to stop such things happening, and all he can offer us is solidarity and support, and stand with us, offering his sympathy. But he is as much a victim of natural disasters as we are. It is truly astonishing that Christian leaders should teach such an extraordinary thing—that God is weak. Everybody knows that 'God (is) Almighty' because the term is all too commonly used as a meaningless expletive, expressing surprise and astonishment. Yet if it is true that God is almighty (and good), we have this problem: Why, given that he is almighty and good, does he allow a natural disaster to occur? Why does he cause it? Why does he not stop it?

Now we will turn to the Bible. Up to this point in our discussion we have not referred to it a great deal, but I am a Christian and this is my authority. I believe it to be the word of God, and I believe it gives the best explanation of things — better than any other writings or any religion. I find it gives the best explanation of our universe—how it came to be, and how it will end. The Bible gives the best explanation of why we are here. It gives the best explanation about the future and, above all, it has quite a lot to say about natural disasters. I am so glad it is a book about facts. It is about God – the living God.

There was a movement some years ago which maintained that God is dead. But people who believed that were not saying that he had ceased to exist. They were saying he was no longer around. He may be alive in some other universe but he is not active in our world now. He used to be, but is not now. But in fact the Bible tells us that God is active here and now in our little world of time and space. That is why there is so much history in the Bible, and so much geography. It is about real people in real time and in real space. Today we can still go and see places mentioned in the Bible. It is a book of reality, and in fact it claims to tell us what God has said and done in our world. That is what we mean by a living God — one who is as active (and speaking) as we are in this world. The Bible is a record of his words and deeds, his miracles and his message to us. So we have here a book in which we can get to know God, and it actually claims to tell us about the only true God. We have already noticed that in Hebrew and Greek, the two languages in which the Bible was written, the word 'true' is the same as our word 'real'. What is real is true, and what is true is real. So it is claiming to tell us about *the only real God* — the only one who really exists. It tells us what he is really like. That is the point on which we now need to focus: 'What is God really like?'

Let us think about what the Bible says concerning

nature. It does not say anything about tsunamis, but then it is about what happened on land, not what happened in the oceans (with one possible exception, which I will mention later). But it does talk about the cause of tsunamis. It has a lot to say about earthquakes, many of them happening within the historical records covered by this book. That is largely because most of the Bible is written about events in an earthquake zone. The biggest crack in the earth's crust stretches all the way from Syria right down through the land of Israel, on down through what is called the Arabah, to the Red Sea. It continues along the Gulf of Acaba, across into Ethiopia, splitting Ethiopia in two; then into Uganda and Kenya, where it splits into two then joins up again and finishes in Mozambique. That is actually the biggest crack in the earth's crust, but actually it is two cracks, and the land between the two cracks has sunk. That is what creates the great Rift Valley as we call it, and it is constantly subject to earth tremors and major earthquakes. So it is not surprising that the Bible is full of earthquakes. It is right in the worst place for the earth to be shaken.

Now some of the earthquakes mentioned are simply natural events. But a number of them we call supernatural events because they have been directly caused by God. That raises the whole question of what is the relationship between God and nature. Does he control everything that goes on in nature — every little breath of wind, every snowflake that falls? Does he switch everything on and off? Not quite. Let us recall and develop a little further our picture of a headmaster and the school timetable. At the beginning of term the headmaster may map out the school timetable and say that every Tuesday morning at ten o'clock it will be French. But, being headmaster, he has the power and the authority to step in on any day and change the timetable and make it do something else. So he can step in on any Tuesday and say it will not be French at ten o'clock, it will be mathematics. Now, roughly speaking, that is how the Bible pictures the relationship between God and nature. He has made a timetable for nature, and, on the whole, he leaves nature to go along that timetable (or what we call the laws of nature) but he has the power and authority to step in at any moment and change that. When he does so, we call the results miracles.

Now that is why we say some of the earthquakes and tremors in the Middle East are due to God stepping in. They are supernaturally controlled rather than simply nature controlled —and they are always linked with some crucial and significant event in the history of God's chosen people. For example, we have an earthquake destroying Sodom and Gomorrah. That was a 'natural' but also a supernatural event. It was God acting in anger, actually destroying not just two but four cities in that earthquake. Then we have another earthquake when God appeared to Moses on the top of Mount Sinai and gave the Ten Commandments. This was a crucial moment. The people of God were camping at the foot of the mountain and were told not to come anywhere near. 'This is holy ground. Moses, you can come and talk with me but don't let the people near.' One of the things that kept them away was an earthquake that shook the mountain, as well as fire and smoke, which seems to indicate a volcanic eruption of some kind. This was God's power being demonstrated. This was God being God, and the fear of God came upon the people.

Then as we move on we find other earthquakes. We

find one during the days of king Saul, and in the time of the prophet Elijah. The biggest one was during the reign of a king called Uzziah, the most severe earthquake in the Old Testament days. The prophet Amos saw this clearly as God's judgement on the people. They were misbehaving very badly and it was God making them pay for it, reminding them of how they were meant to live. It is interesting that centuries later one of the other prophets, Zephaniah, still talked about that earthquake.

When we turn to the life of Jesus we find that the whole universe seemed to be affected by his coming. When he was born there was a star in the sky marking his birth. People have said to me, 'Isn't that astrology? Doesn't that support astrology?' I say not. Astrology believes that the position of stars at a baby's birth affects the baby's character. But in Bethlehem it was the position of the baby that was affecting the stars. That is very different.

When Jesus died, the sun was eclipsed out for three hours and the earth shook. The cross was put in a socket in the rock, and at a certain point the rock shook and shook the cross. It was that which made a Roman army officer who was present say, 'Truly this must have been the Son of God' —because he recognized God reacting to his Son's crucifixion by shaking the rock in which the cross stood. Three days and three nights later the most amazing event happened, which has never happened before or since to another human being. Jesus came back to life with a new body. Again it says there was an earthquake that marked that event. God was marking the event in nature, to emphasise its importance.

As we turn the pages of the New Testament we find Paul and Silas in prison, and they are singing hymns at midnight. They are still praising God even though they are in a pitch black dungeon chained behind locked doors. How did God respond to their praise? He shook the city, the doors of the prison burst open, and Paul, Silas and other prisoners could just walk out. That led to the conversion of the jailor. He had never seen anything like it. He was in utter shock over the whole thing. But at least it opened his heart to think about God.

The Bible ends by predicting an increasing number and scale of earthquakes, which will be of increasing strength. The end of this age will finish with the biggest earthquake there has ever been, which will shake every part of the earth. The Bible then attributes some of the earthquakes that happen in those days to God's direct intervention —to demonstrate his power or express his anger, or simply to mark his presence with them, showing that the God who made it all is now here with his people.

A display, then, of his anger or his power or whatever. We call this theism — when *God controls what he has created*. So some may be called natural and others may be supernatural (what the insurance agents call an 'act of God'). Now we need to ask some very honest questions at this point. Let us state the problem again. If God is almighty, all-powerful and all-loving, and the only God, then frankly we have a big problem. Why then does he cause (or even just allow) such natural disasters, which take a terrible toll of life and cause unlimited damage? Why? Well, we have already seen that we must accept that God is all-powerful according to the Bible. He could start such things and he could stop them. So then why does he do it? Well, we must then turn to the other assumption, that God is all-loving. And we must seriously question that. I know that for a hundred years the church has been focusing on God's love in public preaching. The message we have given to the world is: 'God is love and God loves you'. I am going to show that I believe that has been a terrible mistake, and that we should not have been doing that. I want to apologize for all the preachers who have told you 'God is love and God loves you'.

Now that may be a shocking statement to some readers, but let me back it up. When we turn to the Bible and ask what is God really like, we find some rather surprising facts. I want to give them to you. They will really make you think, and I do not apologize for that. We are to love God with all our minds as well as all our hearts and strength, and the greatest unexplored territory in the world is between your ears. Very few of us are using the brains God gave us to their full capacity and finding out the truth. So what is the truth about God? For a hundred years, as I have said, Christian preachers have been preaching the love of God, and I want to ask: how has that message been heard? How has it been received? What has it conveyed to the people who heard it? My answer, in simple terms, is that it has led to a sentimental view of God rather than a scriptural view. It has led people to construct their own image of God in their imagination, rather than accepting the image of God that is in scripture. Let me tell you what I mean. When we say God is loving, how does the world receive that message? I will tell you. They receive it as meaning that God is so loving that he would never ever cause pain or suffering to anyone — would not hurt a fly; that God loves us so much that he is there to protect us from all pain and suffering and to provide for all our needs; that, in a word, he is there to make us happy. Of course to be really happy you need at the least two things: health and wealth. So it is assumed that God is there to save us from disease and poverty, and that he should not allow anything to come near us that causes us pain, but that he should concentrate on giving us those things that give us pleasure.

So God is there to keep pain away from me and to give pleasure to me. This is the concept that talking about a 'loving God' seems to leave in the minds of many people. He is there to serve us in this way. And frankly, if he does not do that, we fire him. We give him the sack. We say, 'I've called it quits with God.' I have met so many people who talk like that. They say, 'I would believe in God if he hadn't allowed this to happen to me or to my family' — or to my relatives, or to my friends, or to whoever. So they call it quits with God. They say, 'If God does not keep pain and suffering away from me, and give me pleasure and comfort and safety, then I'm finished with God.'

Now that is what many people think when I say that God is a loving God. So I have stopped saying it, because that is not the Bible picture of God. In fact it is a long way from the biblical picture of God. In the Bible he does cause pain and suffering. He does not just give us comfort and safety and pleasure. That is not the true God.

The picture of God in the Bible is not what we like to think he is like. The Bible calls that kind of thinking idolatry, because an idol is an idea of God that you have made for yourself, that you have thought up, whether you make it in wood or stone or just in your own mind. I could make up a God and say, 'That is the kind of god I think should be God; that's the kind of god I like; that's the kind of god I want to be God.' But we cannot manipulate God. God is what he really is, and we have to find out what he really is before we make this kind of guess about his nature. So let us turn to the Bible. No wonder, if we have this sentimental view of God, we have problems when natural disasters occur. That is why we say: 'Why does he allow it? People suffering? He shouldn't be doing that if he's a loving God.' So before we really get an answer to the question we are discussing, we need to ask what is God really like.

So we turn to the Bible, and I begin with what the Bible says about God's love. Here we have some surprises. In all this, please do check in your own Bible; check me out on everything I say. I do not want you to accept my opinion, I want you to find whether what I am telling you is in your Bible. If it is, you can say 'It is the Bible that told me.' Don't say, 'David Pawson told me.' I am just sharing my understanding of the Bible, but I want you to check it all out. Go to your Bible. Read it. Study it, and find out if I am telling you the truth about this, which I believe to be God's word.

I want to make a little point here. You can prove anything you like from the Bible if you take little bits out of it. Take an odd verse here and an odd verse there. You can really prove anything you like, but I am talking about taking the Bible as a whole — the whole picture of God as it is presented in the whole Bible.

Here is the first surprise for you. The Bible says very, very little about the love of God. It does actually mention it, but out of thirty-five thousand verses in your Bible no more than around thirty-five talk explicitly and directly about his love. That is a tiny percentage. The majority of the books in the Bible never mention God's love at all, and the ones that do mention it in only one or two verses. Genesis says nothing about the love of God. Exodus has one verse. Leviticus nothing. Numbers nothing. Deuteronomy has two verses. Joshua nothing. Judges nothing. 1 and 2 Samuel nothing. 1 and 2 Kings nothing. So I could go on. There really are very few references to God's love in the Bible. Why, then, has the church made this its overall message? I think it is because we have fallen for the temptation of telling people what they want to hear rather than telling them the truth.

If the first surprise when we look at the Bible is that there is very little about the love of God, the second surprise is this: that, in fact, it was never talked about in public. Whenever the Jews of the Old Testament talked about God's love, they talked to other Jews. They never talked to any others about it. The Jewish prophets said an awful lot about other nations, but they never said anything about God's love to them. It was a kind of 'in' talk, among Jews only. When we get to the New Testament, we find the same thing is true of Christians talking about the love of God. They never talked about the love of God to those who were not Christians. It was something they kept among themselves. Now that is a big surprise, when the church today is talking about little else to everybody. But neither Jesus nor his apostles ever preached the love of God in public. Take the Acts of the Apostles. That is a book about how the early church evangelized — how the church spread across the Mediterranean world; how they preached to Jew and Gentile, and many came in to faith. Yet not one verse in the Book of Acts ever mentions the love of God. How striking that the early church grew and spread without ever mentioning the love of God!

So that is the second surprise. Why, then, did Jews and Christians only talk among themselves about the love of God, so that every mention in scripture is in private conversation and not in public preaching? The answer is very simple. Both Jews and Christians had been rescued by God. He had done something for them that he has not yet done for anybody else. And they were so grateful; knowing that they were totally undeserving of what he had done, they now understood what love God must have for them. In other words, only those who have been rescued by God (or, in biblical language, those who have been redeemed) can understand what kind of love God has.

That brings me to a third fact in our Bible, which is that they were very careful to use special words for love when they were talking about God, different words from those used of human love. Let me give you a little Greek lesson. I am sorry to get technical, but the Greek language had three different kinds of words for love. We do not need to go into that technically, but they are *eros*, *phileo* and *agape*. These were three different kinds of love, two of which most human beings understand, but the third very few do. The third word was rarely used in the ancient world because it was almost an unknown kind of love, and the Christians seized on that word to describe the love of God to show how different it was from ours.

Let me just run through the three words *eros*, *phileo* and *agape*. *Eros* is primarily a word of the heart, a word of the emotions. It is a love of *attraction* — when you see somebody else and you are attracted to them. This is why that word is so often used of sexual love. It is a love of attraction. Eyes meet across a room. It is an involuntary kind of love. You fall into it, and fall out of it too. It is something you cannot help. Your heart takes over and you fall in love.

Then we come to *phileo*. This is a love of *affection*, not so much a love of attraction. There is a bit of attraction in it, but it is an affection, and primarily love of the mind. Two minds meet and find they have a lot in common, and people become friends. It is partly involuntary, because you meet someone and you are attracted to their mind. You have some things in common. But it is also a voluntary love, because you choose your friends and you can choose whom you go any further with or someone you drop.

Then we come to *agape*, which is a love of *action*. It is doing something good to help someone else. It is a love of the will, and it is entirely voluntary — something that you *choose to do*. When you meet someone in need you can ignore the need or you can choose to do something to help them. That is the kind of love that God has. That is agape love.

To illustrate this, when somebody came to Jesus one day and said, 'How can I love my neighbor . . . what is loving your neighbor?' he told the story of the good Samaritan. A Jew had fallen among thieves and had been beaten up. He had been mugged, and was lying bleeding, in the middle of the road. A priest came walking by and walked past him. Another walked past him. But there was a Samaritan, who normally did not like the Jews at all, and the Jews did not like him. There was no love of attraction for a bleeding Jew lying in the middle of the road, in the heart of the Samaritan. There was no love of affection. The Jewish minds and the Samaritans' minds were so different in their thinking. There was no mutual affection. They disliked each other. But the Samaritan did something good to meet that man's need. That is what Jesus calls love. It is not a love of attraction or a love of affection —that you *like* someone. It is not lusting after someone or liking them, it is doing something to help them. That is practical love, love in action.

In Piccadilly Circus in central London, there is a statue. Do you know what it is called? No, it is not *Eros*. That is not its name. It has been called that because people, looking not too closely at the figure on the statue, think it is Cupid with a bow and arrow, so of course they call it 'Eros'. The love (or even lust) of attraction, particularly sexual. Of course, what goes on around Piccadilly Circus and Soho nearby really fits that. But that statue has nothing to do with eros, that kind of love. It is an 'agape' statue! It was erected to a man called Anthony Ashley Cooper, better known as Lord Shaftesbury, who spent his whole life helping the poor, helping to improve working conditions in factories and coal mines, helping to relieve need. He was greatly admired. So much so that you will find his name in Westminster Abbey. He was admired by the whole country, and his funeral was attended by so many distinguished people because they recognized love in action in him. He did so much good for social welfare all his life. He had been born in the aristocracy, into a rich family, but he spent his life for the poor, for the underdog, for the working class. So they put up this statue, and if you go and read the inscription on the statue you will find anything but eros and anything but phileo, but you will find a lot of agape. This man expressed the kind of love that God has.

Here are the surprises in the Bible about God's love. It is hardly ever mentioned. It is only mentioned among those who have experienced God's action in redeeming and rescuing them from slavery (either in Egypt or slavery to sin, which is far worse slavery and most of us are in it). To put it in a nutshell, those who have experienced forgiveness are those who understand God's love. The one thing the Bible never says is 'God loves everybody'. I challenge you to find a single statement in the Bible that God loves everybody.[1] But the church has been teaching this. No wonder we get such comeback, questions such as 'Why does God allow suffering?' or, 'How can a loving God ever send anybody to hell?' We have invited these challenges. We have created the problem by telling people that God is all-loving and loves everybody. This is not the Bible.

Note

[1] Some viewers took exception to this statement and without exception objected: 'What about John 3:16?' I have answered that in a companion publication to this, entitled *Is John 3:16 the gospel?*

4

DO WE DESERVE DISASTERS?

The Bible says many things about God that really do not sound very 'loving' at all. For example, it says he is very patient with people and he is slow to anger, but he can get very angry with people, and I tell you, when God gets very angry with someone they had better get out of his way. It would be better if they had never been born. My New Testament tells me that it is a fearful thing to fall into the hands of the living God.

Then take another contrast. God is delighted with some people, especially when they are good, but he gets disgusted with other people, and his disgust is written into the Bible. It is called an 'abomination' to him. God can get disgusted with people. The Bible tells us that he gets disgusted with us when we confuse male and female; that he made us to be different, with different roles and different responsibilities; that even different dress and different hairstyles are his will. When we confuse all that, and men behave like women, and women behave like men, and men dress like women, and women dress like men, and when men have sex with men and women with women, the teaching of the Bible is that we are going right against God's provision of the most beautiful thing in our lives — sex. When God made sex, he said, 'Now that is very good.' That was his masterpiece. Male and female he made us, and we are messing up his creation, and God gets disgusted with us for doing this.

Take another contrast. The Bible says that God blesses people and that he curses people. A God who blesses and curses. Is this 'loving' — to curse people? Not in the sentimental mode it isn't. In Deuteronomy 28, God tells the people of Israel, 'I will bless you if you live my way but I will curse you if you don't' and subsequently they experienced both.

So we learn from the Bible that God is patient, but he can get very angry; that he loves and he hates; that he blesses and he curses. Do you know that there are the same number of verses in the Bible about God's hate as about God's love? There are about thirty references to the love of God and thirty references to his hate. The surprising thing is this. You might expect that what he would hate would be evil, but there is no such thing as evil. Evil only exists in evil persons, and out of the thirty references to God's hate, ten (or one-third) refer to his hatred of evil, while two-thirds specifically state that he hates wicked people. I wonder if you have heard the cliché 'God hates sin but loves the sinner'. That is not biblical. He hates sinners too, if they cling to their sin and will not be separated or rescued from it. So God hates people as well as loving people. Therefore, finally God destroys people as well as heals them. He is a God who can heal us, and he is a God who can kill us. And he has killed many, many people according to the Bible. But the important thing is that he always has a good reason for killing.

Before I say more about that, let us just look at this apparent contradiction: that God is patient, slow to anger, but he can get very angry; that he blesses and he curses; that he loves, and he hates; that he heals, and he kills. The Bible gives a very balanced picture of those two sides of God's character. Does that mean that God is good and bad at the same time? Does it mean he is moody — and that you have to catch him in a good mood when you pray to him? Does it mean he is schizophrenic? No. What is it that binds these two sides of his activity together in perfect harmony and consistency? You cannot say love does because many of those things are very 'unloving' in *our* understanding of love. But what binds them together? The answer is that everything can be explained provided God is good. But how good is God? We cannot imagine, because actually you and I have probably never met a really good person. We have met people who are a mixture of good and bad, some more one and some more the other, but no-one is good like God. In fact one day someone came to Jesus and said, 'Good master, what must I do to inherit eternal life?' And Jesus came straight back with, 'Why do you call me good? No-one is good but God.'

Why does God hate? Why does he kill? Why does he curse? Because he is so good! That does not make sense to us because we do not experience perfect goodness, and therefore it is way above our thinking. But God is so good that he has to hate evil. He is so good that he has to curse people who are not good. He is so good that he has to destroy people who are wicked. And in fact that explains many of the incidents in the Bible. Take Noah's flood, for example. The human race began to get worse and worse. We are told in scripture that two things were happening: first of all perverted sex, and, secondly, violence filled the earth. In the saddest verse in the Bible, God said, 'I regretted that I had made man.' I have heard parents say, 'We wish we'd never had children. When the kids are so rebellious and so 'anti' their parents, we wish we'd never had them.' God wished that once. He regretted that he had made man.

So he resolved to destroy them, and he destroyed all that generation. It was an awful thing, but God was cleaning up his earth of those who were polluting it morally. He had created a good earth, put good people on it, but he had given them the freedom to become bad people, and they had done just that. So he reached the end of his patience. He said, 'I'm not going to go on struggling with them', and one thing he said: 'I can see into their minds and everything I see is horrible. Their thoughts are only evil continually. They are constantly thinking bad things.' There was one good family, however. At least there was one good man and his wife, and three sons and three daughters-in-law, and they were good people. God said, 'I'll save that family because they are good. But I have to destroy the others because I am so good that I cannot tolerate their badness.'

The same was true when the Israelites came into Canaan. People say that God is guilty of 'ethnic cleansing', because he told the Israelites to kill all the Canaanites. But we are told that God had waited three hundred years until the Canaanites were so wicked that they did not deserve to live. (Genesis 15:16).

In other words, it is because God is so good. But the word 'good' is losing its meaning. We talk about a good dog, a good holiday, a good meal, good weather. What we mean is that it gives us pleasure. But the word 'good' really should only be used of God, because he is the only really good person in the entire universe. That is why he has to deal with evil. So the word 'good' is really not very helpful to use of God, and the Bible uses another special word. It is in the English dictionary but I rarely hear people use it. It is the word 'righteous'. ***God is righteous.*** That word means that everything he does is right. He is perfectly, absolutely just and fair. You cannot bribe him. You cannot corrupt him. You cannot manipulate him. He will always do what is absolutely right and just. It is good to have a God like that, isn't it?

Or is it? The negative side of his righteousness means that he cannot ever do anything wrong. He cannot tell a lie. He cannot break a promise. He cannot tell a dirty joke. There are so many things God cannot do, and that qualifies his power, because he cannot use that power in a bad way. It is against his whole nature. So here we have a picture in the Bible of a righteous God who will therefore always deal righteously with us. And he must therefore, according to his righteous nature, always punish evil. He would be less than good, less than righteous, if he overlooked badness, if he never punished evil. He has got to do it. He is so good that he will not let anyone get away with bad things. Again, I think that is good news. It means we live in a universe which is moral, that nobody will get away with anything. I know that crime pays now, that two-thirds of crime will not be detected by the police and therefore not punished in the courts — and many criminals think they have got away with it. But take note: God is righteous! Nobody will ever get away with anything. Sin, vice and crime all have to be paid for because this universe is in the hands of a righteous God.

Well now let us begin to draw this section of our discussion to a conclusion. There are two things I could say about God which may cause you to think deeply, and here is the first. A righteous God cannot forgive without a penalty being paid, or he is less than righteous. He must deal with bad things. He must punish them and one day banish them. I can tell you that God has decided to do that. He has already set a day in his diary when he will call every human being to account, and he will punish those who have done bad things and reward those who have done good things. Now how does that grab you? The funny thing is that it is a human weakness that we always think it is somebody else who is bad — that other people are the cause of all the problems in the world, and all the trouble. People say to me, 'Why doesn't God destroy all the bad people now? Why doesn't he get on with it and get rid of all the evil people in the world?' There is an assumption behind that which I find amusing. People are virtually saying, 'and then the rest of us can live happy, safe, comfortable lives'. But I tell you this solemnly, that if God did it now and destroyed everybody who is making this world a worse place than it is, there would not be anybody left. You would have no writer writing this book, and nobody would be reading it, because if God had dealt with me as I deserve I would not be living — and it is not because I am terribly bad. But I know I am polluting his world. So there is the first thing I want to say in conclusion. ***God, being righteous, cannot forgive sin — unless it has been paid for already; unless the penalty for*** *being bad has already been taken by someone else.*

Now that begins to open up a bit of understanding I hope, for you. If God said to you and to me: 'Well, boys will be boys, I'll let you off this time. Try not to do it again', that would be immoral. That would be unrighteous. It would be unfair. It would be unjust. A righteous God could not say that to me. What he could say to me is this: I'll forgive you because somebody else has already paid the penalty for you.

The other thing I want to say in conclusion is this: A righteous God could not punish the innocent, only the guilty — and that raises the whole question of what we really deserve. Do I deserve to live or to die? Do any of us deserve to die? Do any of us deserve to live? These are the questions that I want to deal with in the next chapter. But again this opens up the thought: if God punishes the guilty, why did his only Son die a violent and premature death? A violent and premature death is not deserved by an innocent victim, and if there ever was an innocent person it was Jesus. Even his enemies admitted they could not find anything wrong. Yet God imposed on him a violent and premature death.

5

WILL THEY EVER CEASE?

Again, we think of the central issue. When we consider any major natural disaster, we naturally ask: what did this have to do with God? The question can be put like this. If there is one God, and he is all-powerful and all-loving, how could he allow such a dreadful thing to happen? In the last chapter I suggested that we may need to revise our idea of God. I am giving an answer to this whole question from the Bible, because I believe that is God's word, and it gives us the clearest explanation of all our biggest questions. When we were looking at whether God is all-powerful, we decided the answer has to be yes, he is. He created nature, he is in control of nature, so he could have stopped it. And he could have started it. Yet, even so, we remember there are some things that God cannot do: he cannot tell a lie; he cannot break a promise. I once made a list of the things that God cannot do, and came to thirty very quickly, yet when I read the list again I found that I had done most of the things that God cannot do! That does not make me any more powerful than he is.

But now we are going to consider further the other side of the matter. We asked whether God is all-loving as well as all-powerful, and I was trying to say that this is a misleading term to apply to God because we interpret it in a sentimental rather than a scriptural way. We found that God does things which nobody would say were loving. Yes, he pardons people, but he punishes them; he blesses people, but he curses them. He heals people and he kills people.

We have asked whether that means God has two sides to his character (a good side and a bad side), or whether it means that he is moody, and you have to catch him in a good mood if you want good things from him (he might be in a bad mood). We have seen that it does not mean any of those things. I have been trying to show you that God is so good that he has to do all this. He is so good that he hates evil and even hates evildoers. There is as much in the Bible about God hating as there is about God loving. It is because he is so good, yet we have seen that even the word 'good' is debased today. And we recalled another biblical word for God, namely 'righteous'. **God is so righteous he cannot do anything wrong and everything he does is right.** He can be totally relied upon to be just; to be fair, above manipulation, above bribery, above corruption. He is absolutely good, absolutely righteous. And that explains a number of things about him. As I have studied my Bible I have come to the conclusion that the God I know loves righteousness more than people. That may come as a bit of a shock to you, but you go into your Bible and see if it is true. When he has to choose between sacrificing righteousness or sacrificing people, he chooses people.

We have seen the proof of that in the story of Noah's

flood, a classic example of God loving righteousness more than people because Noah's generation, it says, were unrighteous. They were living for food, drink and sex; they were already into violence; and, finally, God saw that all their thoughts, all the time, were evil. So he destroyed them all in the flood. By the way, that was probably a tsunami as well as rain. It says the 'flood gates of heaven' opened and the rain came down, but it also says that the waters of the great deep welled up — and that surely means a tsunami; there must have been earthquakes as well at that time.

I want you to recall a number of things. First, there was one righteous family. A righteous man called Noah had passed on the right way of living to his family, and eight people were saved from that dreadful disaster. Second, I want you to remember that the flood was deserved. God is so good that he would never send anything on people that they did not deserve. That would be totally unjust and unfair, and God is so good that he would never be unfair. Let me underline that: *they deserved it and he sent it.* Third, I want you to notice also that he gave them ample warning that he was going to do it. So they had no excuse whatever for ignoring what was going to come.

Let us move on from this now. Jesus held a low view of human nature. He said, for example, 'If *you* then, *being evil*, know how to give good gifts to your children . . . .' He is acknowledging that human nature is basically evil, even if we manage to do some good things in our lifetime. It is also said that he would never trust anybody *because he knew what was in man.* That is an extraordinary statement. Jesus would not trust people, could not trust them, because he knew them inside out, and therefore knew what they were really like.

We recall that when the man said to him, 'Good master, what must I do?' he said, 'Why do you call me good? There is no-one good but God' — so really we should never use that word of anybody else. Now this is the very opposite of the humanist viewpoint. Humanists believe that human nature is basically good, even if we do bad things, and humanism often goes on to believe that evil comes to us from outside, that the environment we are in makes us behave badly, but basically we are good. But evil comes from the inside out. The environment can be good, and still people can be bad. Poverty may exacerbate this situation, poverty and bad environment in the family may encourage us to behave badly, but it is only releasing something that is already in there. You know, I had three children, and in fact they learned the word 'no' before they learned the word 'yes'. We never had to teach them how to be cruel to each other, only how to be kind. We never had to teach them how to be rude, only how to be polite. Were our three children worse than anybody else's? No. They were typical. As one mother said to me about her little baby boy: 'It's not his willpower that's the problem, it's his won't power.' She was saying something that every parent knows. Children are not innocent. That is why there is so much bullying in school. That is why we have such problems in the playground. What I am saying is that the Bible has a much higher view of God than we have, and a much lower view of ourselves than we usually have. And that leads to some very interesting conclusions in the word of God.

But before I come to those conclusions, let us look at some of the ways in which we are bad. How bad are we?

I am not talking about real criminals. Everybody thinks some people are wicked: Adolf Hitler, Saddam Hussein. If I said they are going to hell, I think I would be cheered. I certainly would not get some of the letters I have had about these matters, but we all think the wickedness is in someone else, not in us. As I have mentioned, when sometimes people say to me, 'Why doesn't God take all the bad people out of the world and leave the rest of us to enjoy life in peace and safety?' there is a false assumption behind that statement. If God removed everybody who is bad from this world, there would be nobody here at all. You would not be here, and I would not be here, if God had dealt with us in strict justice.

Now let me mention three aspects of our badness in which we all have a share. First, there is our attitude to God's creation. I am sure you realize that we are destroying the environment on which we depend. We are cutting down the forests that give us oxygen to breathe. Animals are becoming extinct – we are not giving them room, and they were all made by God for his pleasure, and we are cutting them down and down. You know that we are destroying the atmosphere with global warming and now global dimming. It is not just the carbon dioxide in the atmosphere, it is tiny carbon particles from our burning fossil fuel which is already cutting down the light that reaches us from the sun, and our food supply depends on that light. The process of photosynthesis produces our food directly or indirectly. So there is our attitude to God's creation — and we are all involved in this. I sometimes travel on a diesel train, which puffs out carbon dioxide and other pollutants. I also travel in cars, which do the same. We are all damaging God's environment. He gave it to us to care for it, to look after it, and we are just not doing that. We are all contributing tons of rubbish, and landfills all over the place. That is just one aspect in which we are all involved. We are spoiling God's creation.

Secondly, I want us to look at our attitude to each other. We kill far more people than any natural disaster does. A quarter of a million in the tsunami was the worst we have seen in our lifetime, but in two world wars fifty to sixty million people were slaughtered, and we are told that in the former USSR eighty million were done to death. In World War II, six million of God's chosen people were killed, and they did not even declare war on anybody, but they suffered. God called the Jews the apple of his eye – which means actually the iris of the eye, the most sensitive part of your body. When you touch his chosen people, you touch his sensitive spot, the apple of his eye.

Some drink and drive, regardless of the danger they are bringing to other people. We break the speed limit. We are doing things every day that are risking the lives of others.

Above all, one third of the world's population goes to bed hungry, another third is starving, and we in the West are eating so much food that we have problems with obesity even in our children.

You know, when Noah came out of the ark, God promised him that he would always see that the whole human race had enough food, and there is enough food in the world now for everybody to be fully fed. Why aren't they? Partly because some of us are so greedy that we won't share our food with those who need it. It is not God's fault that anybody starves, it is ours, and we must take the blame for it.

We are all killers in principle. The Nazis treated Jews as sub-human; we are guilty of the same error if we treat the Nazis as sub-human. They were human beings just like you and me. The soldiers of Auschwitz who were poisoning hundreds of Jews went home to play games with the children and even sing Christmas carols. They were all human beings, and when you get to know yourself as you really are, when you see yourself in the Bible, as in the mirror, you realize that all of us are capable of such things.

Jesus came along and said something quite devastating. He said that you are a murderer in principle if you have ever wished anybody dead. If you have called someone an idiot, you are a killer. I have counselled people who, when they were children, were told by their own parents, 'You're no good' — and that killed their spirit for the rest of their lives.

So our attitude to our fellow creatures reveals us all as capable of being really bad people.

I have mentioned our attitude to creation and our attitude to our fellow creatures. What about our attitude to our Creator? He has given us a book of instructions for life. He has given us certain rules, which he made for our health and our happiness. What do we do about them? We ignore them. We make up our own rules. Take the exquisite pleasure of sex. God said that if you want the most out of sex, then absolute chastity before marriage, absolute fidelity after marriage, and you will enjoy sex better than anyone else. So what do we do? We ignore both rules and we do it our way. I suppose the essence of our rebellion against God is to get to the end of life and say 'I did it my way.' That is the theme song of sinners.

But I am not just thinking about the rules that God gave us for our own good, for our own happiness and health. I am thinking also of how we treat him as a person. Many people ignore him. They would rather go to a boot sale or a football match on Sunday than spend an hour with his people, thanking him, telling him how much he means to us. We insult him by turning our adoration and worship to other gods — not just other religions necessarily, but other gods such as film stars, pop stars, sporting stars; and we give them the adoration that belongs to God alone. God alone is worthy of such worship.

Above all, we insult him by not thanking him for all that he does for us. I want to pick up one story from the Old Testament that illustrates God as he really is. There were hundreds of thousands of people stuck in a desert called Sinai, and they were there by their own fault. They could have gone into the promised land in fourteen days. They were to spend forty years in the wilderness because they would not trust God – the God who brought them out of Egypt – they would not trust him to get them into the promised land. They did not believe in him. So they were stuck in the wilderness. God could have left them on their own and said, 'You didn't go in and take the land when I gave it to you. You die.' But he didn't, he fed them every day with miraculous food called 'manna', and he gave them water from dry rocks; he fed them and he kept them clothed, and he kept them watered, for forty years. But on one occasion during those forty years they turned on Moses, whom God had used to bring them out of slavery. They grumbled about the food God was giving them. They said it was horrible food; they missed the spices and garlic in Egypt. Why did you bring us out just to give us this horrible food? Now that food had all the minerals, all the proteins, all the carbohydrates, all the vitamins that they needed. But they did not like it, so they grumbled, and God was angry with that.

What did he do about it? He sent venomous snakes in among them, and many were bitten and died. Whole families were touched by these snakes, losing loved ones. So they repented. They cried out to Moses, 'Tell God we've sinned; we shouldn't have done that, we should never have grumbled. Please ask him to take the snakes away.' But he did not take them away. He actually left the snakes there to go on biting and killing them. But what he did do was to tell Moses to put a metal snake up on a pole and put it on a hill at the edge of the camp, and when anybody was bitten they just had to look at that snake on the pole and the venom disappeared from their body.

Now you may say, 'What a horrible story; that's Old Testament stuff, isn't it?' No, it isn't. Jesus himself endorsed that view of God: a God who gets angry when he is not thanked for what he has done to support us in our living. And do you know where in the New Testament that is endorsed by Jesus? John, Chapter 3, verses 14 and 15 — and then comes verse 16, 'For in the same way God loved the world.' In other words, you have got to line up God's love with a God who gets angry enough to kill people when they are ungrateful. When did you last thank God for all he has done to keep you alive? Do you see what I mean? We take it for granted. We say we have a right to food, a right to health, a right to life. No, we haven't.

I have only touched on these three areas, we could go on to think about our attitude to creation, to our fellow creatures and to the Creator himself, but let us now move on to the conclusions that the Bible draws from all this.

The first conclusion the Bible draws is this: *we do not deserve to live.* We are all spoiling God's creation for ourselves, for other people and for him. We are all guilty. None of us is good enough to look after his world. That is the first conclusion and it is a very important one.

The second conclusion is this: *we deserve to die.* Every one of us deserves to die. Why? Because God could not let bad people live forever and spoil his universe forever and ever. So he has put a time limit on how long we can live—seventy or eighty, or maybe nowadays ninety or even a hundred years or so. But then we die. It is an interesting thing: the Bible does not say that death is a natural event. In the Bible, death for human beings is not natural. We were not made to die. We were not intended to die, and we rebel against death. We postpone it as long as possible. We do not talk about it because we were not made to die and we know it. It is an enemy so we try not to talk about it. We do not like facing it. It is the unmentionable subject today, because it is not natural, it is a judicial event. By that I mean that we are guilty and deserve to die, and God has said to us 'You will die.' He told Adam that, right in the Garden of Eden. 'The day you disobey me, you die.' He must put a limit on our lives so that we do not go on spoiling things for ever and ever. He had to do it. So any death, whether early or late, is a judicial event; or, to put it bluntly, it is an execution of someone who does not deserve to live.

I am going to go one step further. Not only do we not deserve to live, and not only do we all deserve to die, but *we all deserve a premature and violent death.* We might accept death if it came peacefully and in old age when we are tired and ready to go to sleep, but we actually all deserve a premature and violent death. What makes me say that? Well, as a Christian I believe there was one person who did not deserve to die. There has only been one good life lived in the entire history of the world, and nobody can argue otherwise. Even his enemies admitted they could not find a fault, and of course I am talking about Jesus. Jesus, therefore, should have gone on living for ever. But he didn't, and God arranged for him to die — not peacefully, at the age of seventy or eighty, in his bed in Nazareth, but it was an execution at the age of thirty, a particularly painful, humiliating death — strung up on a stake, just like that snake on the pole that Moses put up. And because he died a violent and premature death, and because I know that God planned that, and that he planned it so that he could die in my place and pay the price that I deserve to pay, then I know that I deserve a violent and premature death. That is why every Christian regards any day of living, any life, whether short or long, as a *mercy*, an **undeserved favour of God**.

I was once interviewing an undertaker, and I said to him, 'You must have been in many homes where there has been a tragic, sudden, unexpected death. Some would have been Christian. Did you ever notice any difference between a Christian home that faces a sudden, premature death and non-Christian homes?'

He looked very thoughtful for a long time, and then he said, 'Yes, I've noticed one difference. In Christian homes there is no bitterness, no resentment.' I realized that he was giving a real tribute to Christians. Christians know that we all deserve to die prematurely, that we all deserve to die violently, and that therefore anything other than that is a sheer undeserved mercy of God.

In the middle of the Bible it says this: *It is of his great love that we are not consumed* (Lamentations 3:22). Now this is throwing a whole different light on the question. The Bible never asks the question that I am dealing with in this book. The Bible never says, 'Why did God allow this to happen?' In fact, the Bible leads us to the opposite question, a very different question. It is not, 'Why did so many die in that natural disaster?', but, 'Why did so few die?' Not, 'Why do natural disasters come from time to time?', but, 'Why don't they come more often?' If this is what we really deserve, then the amazing thing is that they do not happen more often and kill more people. That is a totally different viewpoint. How have we got to that viewpoint? Because the Bible is telling us that God is far better than we thought he was, and that we are far worse than we thought we were. The whole picture changes when you get a biblical viewpoint.

Let Jesus have a word on this. Jesus lived to see a disaster. A tower fell, much as the towers in New York collapsed. Now we don't know whether the tower that fell in Jesus' day had a natural cause or a human cause. Was it a bad bit of building? Or was it an earthquake? Or was it even a mixture of the two — that it was not strong enough to withstand tremors in what is a well-known earthquake zone? Whatever the cause, whether it was natural or human, it was a disaster of great proportions, and many people lost their lives. Some people came to Jesus and said, 'Were the people who died in the disaster worse than us, worse than the survivors?' In other words, was the disaster targeted to get rid of people who were worse than others?

Jesus' answer was very simple. He said no, they were not worse, but they were no better either. Jesus' answer says this: they deserved it, and so do you, and you have been given an opportunity to put things right before you die. 'Unless you repent, you will all likewise perish' (Luke 13:3).

Now that is quite an answer. You see, I am a follower of Jesus. I believe he was the truth. I believe he spoke the truth. And when he said about that disaster that the people who died in it deserved to die, and so do the survivors, I believe he was speaking the truth, and that should be our reaction at any natural disaster or human disaster, however it is caused. *They deserved it and so do we. Thank God for his mercy in giving me a chance to put things right before I go the same way.* Because one thing is sure, we are all going the same way. I am a dying man, so are you. I am in my seventies, my children tease me that I have one foot in the grave and the other on a banana skin, but that is the truth. If a day is your life, I am living after eleven o'clock at night. And we need to be realistic about this. I am going to die and so are you. That I am still alive at my age is a mercy of God, it is not something I deserve. It is not something I have got a right to. It is something that he has allowed me. I could have died very much earlier than this.

The Bible is full of insights which help us to understand things, and here is another insight which may never have occurred to you. Nature and human nature are connected. All are part of God's creation. Now we are increasingly realizing that this is so at a physical level. We realize that what we do is affecting nature, and that what happens in nature affects us. We have already observed that global warming, global dimming, is due to our burning fossil fuels, among other things. So we know now there is a connection between us and nature. What you may not have realized is this: the Bible teaches that there is a moral and spiritual connection between human nature and nature; that at a moral and spiritual level, we affect each other; and that nature is no longer good. It was good when it left God's hand at the beginning, and he looked at nature and said, 'That's good. I am pleased with that.' He had pleasure in it because it was so good. But it is not good now. Somehow, nature has also been affected by this rebellion in us against God. Once upon a time the wolf and the lamb could lie down together in co-existence and safety. Once upon a time, the lion was vegetarian. Once upon a time, snakes were not venomous. That is what it says in my Bible. It has gone terribly wrong, so that not only is human nature bad, but nature is now less than good. So the two are interlinked, and therefore there can be a subtle link between nature going wrong and human nature going wrong, which comes out in disasters.

Now I will come to the biggest surprise of all in a

moment, but the Bible does say that nature herself is struggling or *groaning*. That could be the sound between the tectonic plates, but nature is groaning because nature also needs redeeming, saving, changing, to be brought back into a good state. Surprisingly enough, the Bible says that nature will not be saved and made good again until we have been — that the whole creation is groaning, struggling, waiting for us to be redeemed, and when that happens, nature too will be released from death and decay. (Romans 8:22–23).

That is an extraordinary statement. It is interesting that that word 'struggle' was taken up by Darwin in his theory of evolution. He saw nature as a struggle and the fittest surviving. That was taken up by Karl Marx. He talked about 'struggle' between the bourgeoisie and the proletariat, and the working class were the fittest and would survive. It was taken up by Nietzsche, whose philosophy influenced Hitler, and Hitler wrote a book entitled *Mein Kampf* — My Struggle. The twentieth century was shot through with this word 'struggle' and the 'survival of the fittest'. The word 'struggle' has a tragic history.

Jesus predicted that, towards the end of this phase of our world, there would be a great increase in disasters, whether caused by human beings or nature, so he listed them together. He said there would be wars, famines and earthquakes. (Matthew 24:7). Wars are clearly humanly caused. Earthquakes are nature caused; famines, probably a bit of both. But he is saying that we can expect an increase. Did you know that earthquakes are doubling every ten years? It is not just that we hear about them now, through television and radio. It is that they are on the increase. Ask any seismologist. Jesus predicted this two thousand years ago. Now what is happening? Who is responsible for the increase? More people died, proportionately to the world population, in the twentieth century than in any previous century. What is the twenty-first going to be like? Well, it has already had a bad start, and we are not even over the first ten years yet. Since World War II there have been thirty-six wars which were international conflicts, to say nothing of civil conflicts. These disasters are increasing, which means that pain and suffering are going to increase.

That is what Jesus said. Well, is it coming true? I believe so. But why are they increasing? In very simple terms, I believe it can be explained by the fact that God is taking his restraining hands off nature and off human nature. I suppose we shall never know how much we owe to God's restraint of our sin, crime and vice. He has been restraining it but we read for example in the first chapter of Paul's letter to the Romans about what happens when God takes his hands off human society. There is a great increase in unnatural sexual relations. There is an increase in violence. There is an increase in family break up, and especially children becoming less and less obedient to parents. When you read Romans chapter 1 it is like reading a Sunday tabloid newspaper! All these things happen because God takes his hands off human nature. Why should he do that? Again you will find the simple biblical answer in that very chapter, Romans 1. When men give God up, he gives men up. That is fair, isn't it? That is just. When they pay less and less attention to him, he pays less and less attention to them. They give up worshipping and thanking him; he gives up restraining evil on the earth and in society.

So we have a clear picture here of God taking his hands off human nature, and we see the results of that all around us. Who could argue with Paul's analysis of what happens when God takes his restraining hand off society? But we are told in the Bible that towards the end God will take his restraining hand off nature as well, and therefore it will behave more and more badly. This will build up.

Another shock for us in the Bible is that Jesus himself is sharing this act of God. According to the Book of Revelation, he is breaking the seals on the scroll on which is written the final countdown of our history, and as he breaks the seals he, Jesus, releases warfare, bloodshed, pestilence and death on the human race. We must take that into account when we try to understand the full character and nature of our Lord Jesus Christ.

So we have an expectation in the Bible of a build-up of disasters, whether caused by human or natural causes, or both. Therefore, I am afraid I have to tell you that the Asian tsunami was one of a series that will increase in number and strength, until finally we are told there will be one gigantic earthquake that will shake the entire earth — all the tectonic plates rubbing against each other and releasing tons and tons of energy, both on land and under the water. That is the scenario which my Bible paints, and it is not a very pleasant one, but we shall see whether the Bible has been accurate.

Here is another surprise in the Bible. God has written this world off. It is already beyond redemption. It is already too polluted to recover. He has put a date in his diary for dissolving not just planet earth but the whole universe around it. And he is going to do it the way that Einstein predicted. Einstein's simple formula $e = mc^2$ means, very simply, that the amount of energy packed into any bit of matter (this book, any atom of matter) is the weight of it times the speed of light squared. That is a huge amount of energy. It was that which led directly to the atom bomb and the hydrogen bomb — releasing an incredible amount of energy from a tiny bit of matter. Every cell in the universe, every bit of matter is packed energy, packed there by God, and we are told that whereas once he destroyed a whole world with water, at the end he will destroy it with fire. I have taken it, therefore, that he simply releases the energy that he packed in, and the whole thing burns out.

Now that is not very nice, is it? But there is one remarkable statement on the lips of Jesus, who predicted all this, and it is this: that these horrible sufferings are birth pains, not death pains. Yes, death can be very painful, but birth is painful too. And Jesus said: When you hear of all these disasters increasing, don't be too troubled. They are creation in 'labour' for a new world that's coming. That is a totally different way of looking at increasing disasters, that this is the beginning of a new world. God has already decided to roll up this one and to build a new heaven and a new earth: a new planet earth, and new space around it. Brand new. And the one thing he is going to make quite sure is this — that nothing bad will ever enter it. He has decided to start all over again. He is going to make a brand new universe wherein righteousness resides. In simple terms, nothing and no-one will be allowed to pollute it in any way.

What a vision for the future! You will only find it in the Bible, because that is God telling us what he is going to do. The Bible is a history book, but it is unlike any other history book you will find in the library. It begins earlier and it ends later than any other history book. It begins with the beginning of our world, and it ends with the end of it. At the end of it a new world is born, birthed by the same God who gave us this universe. That is the teaching of the Bible.

Now do you think that is good news? Well, I would not blame you if you said 'I'm not quite sure', because the chances of you getting into that new world are nil if God will not let anybody in who will pollute it in any way — morally, physically, whatever. Then you and I do not stand a chance.

So, in a sense, the Bible ends with very bad news. But just a moment, who is going to inhabit that new world? Who will be fit enough, and how can God prevent it going wrong the same way it went this time? We need to go back to the beginning: 'Why did God create the human race in the first place?' My answer, and it is very simple I am afraid, is this. He already had one Son, and enjoyed him so much that he wanted a bigger family. I cannot put it more simply than that. I believe that is why he created us, to be his sons and daughters — not his *natural* children; he only had one natural Son (or one only-begotten Son, as the Bible puts it), but to be his *adopted* children. He wanted us to be his larger family, sharing his love, sharing the relationship he already had with his Son and with his Spirit. That was the whole concept behind our arriving in the universe, according to the Bible.

71

Others may say we are the result of an accident, we are pure chance, it was luck that put molecules together in the way we have come together. They are welcome to that. I find I would need to have more faith to believe that than to believe that somebody put me here and made me like himself so that I could have relationship with him and fellowship with him.

Let us ask another question. If God has already written off this world – if he is going to start all over again – why does he not get on with it? Why does he destroy the world in little bits? Why does he not just have that one huge disaster, getting rid of us all, and then start again? The answer is this: he does not want to do that. He has no pleasure in destroying what he has made. He hates doing it. He has to do it because he is so righteous, but he hates doing it. He does not enjoy it. He is not a sadist. He is not taking revenge on us, that is not God. He does not want to let us go. He does not want to have to wipe us all out. In fact he has thought up an amazing plan. Supposing he just wiped us all out, made a new universe, made new human beings and put them in it. How long do you think it would be before they went the same way as we have gone? No further than the first generation probably. Or else, supposing he made people for this new universe who could not be bad, who were puppets, who were forced to be good, who were forced to be obedient, forced to keep his laws. That would not be a family because family love can only depend on voluntary choice of people who want to be in that family, people who want to be loved and to love, people who want to be the sons and daughters of their heavenly Father — so that would defeat its purpose. So what is his great plan? It is to take some of us and so change us that we can go into that new world without spoiling it. I could not put it more simply than that. God wants some from every ethnic group in this old world in that new world, because he made every ethnic group. He wants people from every kindred and tribe and tongue on earth in that new world. But he will never force any of us to be in it. He is looking for people who are willing to be changed. The Bible uses the word 'repent' for that, but I am just spelling it out very simply.

God has decided that those who are willing to be changed can go and live in that new universe, and having been in this world already and having seen what happens when it becomes a godless world, and seeing the mess we make it into, those people will never want to see that again. They will have finished with all that. They will want to be good and they will be good.

Now one thing is absolutely sure, and that is this: you and I can never make ourselves good enough for God. People have tried. Most people do not even try. Most people just say, 'Well, nobody's perfect', and accept themselves as they are. They say, 'You can't change human nature.' That is a lie — except that it is true that *you and I* cannot. But God can. And he will. Somebody said that God can do wonders with a broken life provided that he gets all the pieces in his hands. He can put them together again. He can turn sinners into saints. He can turn the wicked into righteous. He can make bad people into good people. That is the gospel I preach. It is the gospel the Bible preaches. It is a gospel of changing human nature so that bad people become good people, and are so grateful that they never want to live in an old world like this again and will want to be good.

Very briefly, this needs the work of three persons: God the Father, God the Son and God the Holy Spirit. The first step is when God says: 'I am going to forget your past. I am going to forgive and forget. I am going to treat you as if you are already totally innocent, as if you are already totally righteous.' We call that *imputed* righteousness, because God actually calls us innocent. He uses the term *justified* or acquitted. It is a law court term. He is saying, 'This person is good in my sight.' I love the New Guinea Pidgen English Bible. It has some vivid phrases, and one of them, where your Bible says 'justified', the Pidgen English Bible says, 'God, 'e say, I'm alright.' Is that not wonderful — that God should look at me and say, 'He's alright; I can't find anything wrong in him'? That is forgiveness. As I have said, it is only possible because Jesus has already paid the penalty. God is so good he could not overlook what I have been and done and said and thought. He could not, he is too good for that. God cannot just let us off, but when somebody else has paid the penalty for us he can treat us as innocent.

But that is only the beginning of change. We are still basically the old person, and the 'old man' will rear his ugly head from time to time. But there is a new man being created, and the third person of the Holy Trinity, the Holy Spirit, is the one who does that. Christ died to pay the penalty for us. The Holy Spirit is going to impart God's righteousness to me. He is going to make me perfect.

My wife has a strong faith, but there is one thing I preach that she finds very difficult to believe, and she tells me so. It is when I tell her that one day her husband will be perfect. Then she says to me, 'If I based my faith on experience, I could not believe that.' But she says, 'I'll try and base it on God's promises.' And God has promised to make me perfect; to restore his image in me; to make me a good man, fit to go into his new world without polluting it, without spoiling it for other people, without spoiling it for him. That is the good news of the gospel of Jesus Christ.

Let us come back to the question of natural disasters. We can now see them from a biblical perspective. If I think of the tsunami, for example, first I do not believe it was targeted. I mean by that I do not believe God chose either a special place or a special time for that tsunami or the earthquake that caused it. I have heard people who do. For example, I have heard some people say it was a chosen place. I heard a Muslim mullah who said that it was particularly targeted by Allah against the sex industry in largely Buddhist Thailand. He conveniently overlooked the fact that Sumatra, a Muslim country, got the worst of it. Then I heard a Christian preacher saying that it was targeted at Sumatra because Christians have suffered so much in Indonesia, of which Sumatra is part. He conveniently overlooked that the worst of the tsunami in India hit the state of Tamil Nadu, which is the most Christian part of India, where 13% of the people are Christian, and in Sri Lanka there were many Christians living along the shore. So I do not think we can say that God targeted this, that he directed its placing to punish particular people. Nor do I believe the timing was carefully chosen. It was Boxing Day, a Christian festival day, and it was full moon day, which of course is linked with Islam, but I do not believe it was targeted in time and place. I believe it was a global warning —that God was reminding us of his justice, that we all deserve disaster, that we all deserve to die, even prematurely and violently.

But it was also a reminder of his mercy, because he is not wiping us all out. He is giving those of us who survive even more time to repent, to think again and get right with him. The real questions we need to be asking ourselves now are these: Why do I cry to God when I am suffering and not when I am sinning? Why do I cry to God in terror but not in temptation? What am I really worried about in my life — my discomfort or my disobedience?

Turning to God and saying, 'God, I need your help; I need you to make me into a good person so that I can live in your new world' — that is when things really begin.

About David Pawson

David Pawson continues the legacy of great British Christian writers. His best known work, _Unlocking the Bible_, is a worldwide best seller in print, audio and video formats.

Pawson is known for accepting biblical text as the authoritative word of God while explaining its meaning and context in a practical and understandable language. Because he follows the teaching of Scripture where it clashes with church tradition, his books are often controversial.

Today David speaks around the world and is received on God TV by millions of viewers in almost every country.

Born in 1930, David determined to become a farmer after completing a B.Sc. in agriculture at Durham University. He was surprised when God intervened and led him into the ministry. Studying for an advanced degree in theology at Cambridge, under the influence of liberal educators, Pawson lost his trust in the Bible and very nearly his faith in God.

He regained his trust in the infallibility and inerrancy of the Bible while a chaplain in the Royal Air Force. During this period he decided to preach the Bible systematically from start to finish. The results among the servicemen surprised both him and them, and confirmed to him Scripture's inspiration. Since then, his preaching has either been Bible study or topical studies based on a detailed, contextual examination of what the Bible says.

As pastor of Millmead Centre, Pawson established a reputation among both evangelicals and charismatics as a Bible expositor. Under Pawson's ministry, Millmead became the largest Baptist church in Britain.

He is a frequent speaker in the UK and throughout many parts of the world, including Europe, Australia, New Zealand, South Africa, The Netherlands, Israel, Southeast Asia and the United States.

David Pawson lives near Basingstoke, Hampshire in southern England with his wife Enid.

Other Books By David Pawson

- Unlocking the Bible

- Israel in the New Testament

- Defending Christian Zionism

- Come With Me Through Revelation

- Practicing the Principles of Prayer

- The Normal Christian Birth - How to Give
  New Believers a Proper Start in Life

- Leadership is Male - What Does the Bible Say?

- Word and Spirit Together- Uniting
  Charismatics and Evangelicals

- The Road to Hell

- Christianity Explained

- The God and the Gospel of Righteousness

- Is John 3:16 the Gospel?

- When Jesus Returns

- Jesus Baptizes in One Holy Spirit

*David Pawson's books are available in North America
through True Potential Publishing, Inc.
For more on David Pawson, sample reading and online
ordering please visit **http://pawsonbooks.com**.*

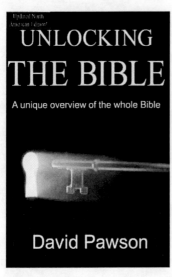

Unlocking
The Bible

by: David Pawson
1119 Pages, Paperback
ISBN # 978-0-9823059-0-4
Cover Price $23.95

Unlocking the Bible brings together a lifetime's worth of insights from David Pawson.

Taking an overview of the unique story of God's relationship with his people, _Unlocking the Bible_ gives a real sense of the sweep of biblical history and its implications for our lives.

The culture, historical background and spiritual significance of all the important events are explained, with careful examination of their wider impact, right up to the present day.

This is a fantastic opportunity to get to grips with the Bible as a whole.

Reviews:

"I cannot think of a better book for new believers to read than this. Motivation to make Bible study more than a just a discipline - a fun hobby."

"Unlocking the Bible" is exactly what this book does. It's not theologically heavy, and you'll find yourself intrigued and desiring more and more of the Bible when you read it!"

"Love, love, love this book. I love David Pawson's style of teaching. Very understandable and simple. This is a great companion to studying the Word."

Come With Me Through Revelation

by: David Pawson
336 Pages, Paperback
ISBN # 978-0-9818961-8-2
Cover Price: $15.99

As a history book the Bible is unique, telling us about the future as well as the past. To become obsessed with either is to evade life's challenges. Both perspectives are needed to live 'over the circumstances' of the present.

The book of Revelation focuses on the future and can produce two reactions among Christians - some cannot get into it and others cannot get out of it! We need a more balanced view of its significance. After all, it is the only book in the whole Bible to which God has attached a special blessing and an awful curse.

It was written for ordinary people under extraordinary pressure. Suffering is the key to its understanding. It is a manual for martyrdom.

As history draws to a close, all Christians need its message of warning and encouragement.

This is the first in a major new series in which David Pawson invites the reader to Come with me through . . . a book of the Bible.

Explore online! You can find reviews, samples and commentary on all of David Pawson's books at ***http://pawsonbooks. com***. David Pawson's books are also available at better bookstores across North America.

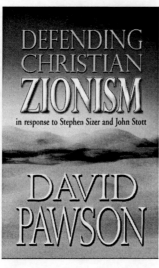

in response to Stephen Sizer and John Stott

Defending Christian Zionism

by: David Pawson
160 Pages, Paperback
ISBN # 978-0-9818961-7-5
Cover Price: $14.99

* Has God brought the Jewish people back to Palestine?

* How can both Jews and Christians be God's chosen people?

* How many covenants are there in the Bible?

* Do all Christian Zionists accept dispensational teaching?

* Does the God of Israel ever change his promises?

These are some of the questions that must be faced in the light of current attacks on Christian Zionism by some evangelical writers. David Pawson believes that Christians need very clear biblical understanding before making political pronouncements about conflict in the Middle East.

"Needless to say, David Pawson is valued as one of the most serious, knowledgeable, insightful and scrupulously sincere Bible teachers of our time. For that reason alone it is well worth taking heed of his thoughts, but, as he always says himself, -judging them for yourself against the light of God's Word."
Reflections (UK)

Explore online! You can find reviews, samples and commentary on all of David Pawson's books at ***http://pawsonbooks.com***. David Pawson's books are also available at better bookstores across North America.

Practicing the Principles of Prayer

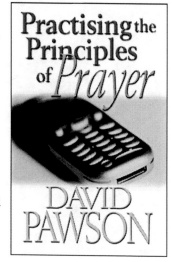

by: David Pawson
281 Pages, Paperback
ISBN # 978-0-9818961-9-9
Cover Price: $14.99

At one time or another we've all prayed for something. Did any of those prayers ever go unanswered? Have you ever wondered why?

What are the seven things you must believe that get answers to prayer? ***Practicing the Principles of Prayer*** covers all seven and much more.

Did you know that according to the Bible:

- you never pray alone
- prayer isn't meditation - it's conversation
- 95% of prayer is talking and asking
- prayer is out loud
- your eyes are open

There are many books on the subject of prayer, but this one is different. It is a clear, practical, biblical guide to prayer. These aspects of the subject are covered in depth:

- Prayer to the Father
- Prayer through the Son
- Prayer in the Spirit
- Prayer against the devil
- Prayer with the saints
- Prayer by myself
- Prayer for others
- Prayer without hindrance

When Jesus Returns

by: David Pawson
269 Pages, Paperback
ISBN # 978-0-9823059-1-1
Cover Price: $14.99

In these days of heightened concern about the end-times, what is really known about Christ's second coming and how can we prepare for it?

Christians everywhere await Christ's return. Will he come to the whole world or just one place? Soon and suddenly or after clear signs? What can he achieve by coming back here and how long will it take?

David Pawson brings clarity and insight to these and many other vital issues surrounding the bodily return of Jesus Christ to our world. Based on a new approach to the interpretation of the book of Revelation, he discusses in detail the controversial and misunderstood subject of the 'Rapture' and uncovers the true significance of the 'Millennium'.

Reviews:

"The book of Revelation made simple! This book clearly and simply pulls together God's eternal plan to dwell with man again forever."

"This study provides clarity and insight to these issues. Highly recommended."

Explore online! You can find reviews, samples and commentary on all of David Pawson's books at ***http://pawsonbooks.com***. David Pawson's books are also available at better bookstores across North America.

The Normal Christian Birth

by: David Pawson
327 Pages, Paperback
ISBN # 978-0-9823059-2-8
Cover Price: $15.99

This is a handbook on spiritual
obstetrics. It is not just for
evangelists, though it is
particularly relevant to their
ministry. It is for pastors, youth
leaders, church workers and,
indeed, all Christians who have a heart to win others for Christ,
all who at some time find themselves 'assisting' when a person
is 'born again'.

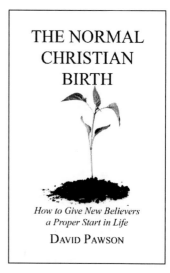

THE NORMAL
CHRISTIAN
BIRTH

*How to Give New Believers
a Proper Start in Life*

DAVID PAWSON

Basically, this book is about how to become a 'Christian'. It is
written out of a burden for a better quality of 'conversion' (as
well as a bigger quantity, which all long to see).

Reviews:

*"If you've read David Pawson you will expect a tightly argued,
clearly and lucidly structured and presented approach from
arguably the best Bible teacher of this generation. This book
is no exception. Clarity of insight and non technical wording
come as standard with Pawson."*

*"This book is destined to become a Christian classic! If you
are a Christian and haven't yet read it do so immediately! It
covers the basics of full 'Christian Birth'."*

Christianity Explained

by: David Pawson
176 Pages, Paperback
ISBN # 978-0-9818961-0-6
Cover Price: $14.99

David Pawson discusses the essential questions of the Christian faith.

- Is there a God?
- Is He a good God?
- Was the death of Jesus murder or suicide?
- Where is He now? What does 'saved' mean?
- How does one become a Christian?
- What about the Holy Spirit?
- Where does the Church fit in? How will it all end?

Reviews:

"Some years ago, when I was looking in hurt for a real God – not just somebody I sang hymns to – two books quickly brought Him into focus. One of the books was this one. What it did, I now believe, was to clear from my confused view all the dense undergrowth we can accumulate through childhood and into manhood. I call this undergrowth 'religion'."

Gerald Williams
Sports Commentator

"A thoroughly readable book offering a condensed and well illustrated survey of basic Christian truths."

Bishop John Perry

Israel in the New Testament

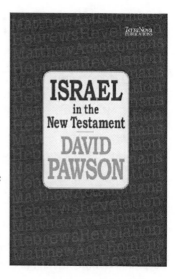

by: David Pawson
315 Pages, Paperback
ISBN # 978-0-9823059-7-3
Cover Price: $14.99

Those who believe what the Bible teaches about God's plans and purposes for the people and place of Israel are often accused of giving more time and attention to the Old Testament than the New, and there is some truth in this.

Over 80% of the promises and prophecies of the Old Testament have been literally fulfilled. It is a simple matter of faith in God's faithfulness to believe that he means what he says, and will do what he says he will do.

This exciting new study reveals that both the people and the place called 'Israel' have a significant role in God's future plans for world redemption.

Five books of the New Testament are used here to illustrate this important truth.

Explore online! You can find reviews, samples and commentary on all of David Pawson's books at ***http://pawsonbooks.com***. David Pawson's books are also available at better bookstores across North America.

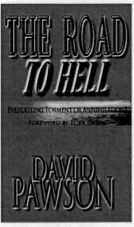

The Road to Hell

by David Pawson

227 Pages, Paperback
ISBN # 978-0-9818961-5-1
Cover Price: $14.99

Challenging 'universalism' and 'annihilationism', Pawson presents the traditional concept of endless torment as soundly biblical, illustrating his argument with in-depth Scripture studies on controversial passages.

'Hell is the most offensive and least acceptable of all Christian doctrines. We try to ignore it but it won't go away. Better to face the truth, even if it hurts.'

Is John 3:16 the Gospel?

by: David Pawson
85 Pages, Paperback
ISBN # 978-0-9818961-1-3
Cover Price: $11.99

David Pawson writes: John 3:16 is often referred to as 'the gospel in a nutshell'. I believe it is one of the most mistranslated and misapplied verses in the Bible. Like most Christians, I totally misunderstood the verse. So I am warning you now that I may spoil John 3:16 for you for the rest of your life. But I hope that this book will also give you the true meaning of what is a wonderful message, and a very important one, especially for Christians.

The God and the Gospel of Righteousness

by: David Pawson

51 Pages, Paperback
ISBN # 978-0-9818961-2-0
Cover Price: $11.99

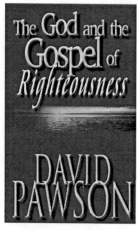

David Pawson calls the church back to the very heart of the good news. For many, the 'gospel' is that God loves everybody unconditionally. Yet neither Jesus nor his apostles ever preached like that. They seem to have thought that the world needed to know about his righteousness and his willingness, even his eagerness, to share that with us. That is because he is determined to have a universe in which there is no unrighteousness whatever. Why don't we think that is good news?

Leadership is Male

by: David Pawson
116 Pages, Paperback
ISBN # 978-0-9818961-3-7
Cover Price: $11.99

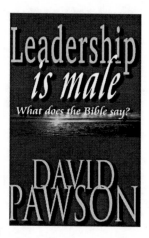

Elisabeth Elliot writes in the Foreword: "Here is a simple, sane, serious treatment of the subject by a man who loves God, respects women, and takes the inspiration of Scripture and the integrity of the apostles for granted. He deals with all the 'difficult' texts. He tells us that his subject is not a clerical issue, nor is it hierarchical, situational, historical, or experimental; it is *biblical.* Read this book. The exegesis points to the mystery. Mysteries are things revealed, not explained. Mysteries are always unsettling."

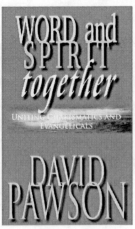

Word and Spirit Together

by David Pawson

227 Pages, Paperback
ISBN # 978-0-9818961-6-8
Cover Price: $14.99

David Pawson has a passionate desire to see Charismatics and Evangelicals united. He has made a searching study of their remaining differences which he believes can be resolved without compromise. This book is essential reading for every Christian with a vision for a church united in faithfulness to the Word and openness to the work of the Holy Spirit.

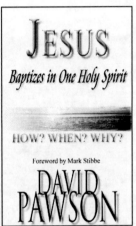

Jesus Baptizes in One Holy Spirit

by David Pawson
227 Pages, Paperback
ISBN # 978-0-9823059-3-5
Cover Price: $14.99

Pawson describes eight essential elements in Spirit baptism. He maintains that the sacramental, evangelical and Pentecostal streams of Christianity have all failed to do justice to this biblical doctrine.

"I strongly recommend this book for those wanting to stretch their traditional way of thinking about salvation and in particular the baptism of the Holy Spirit ...." **P.D. Goulding, Preston, Lancashire, UK**